A BOOK OF POEMS

AL QUE QUIERE!

W. C. Williams in 1917

AL QUE QUIERE!

The Centennial Edition

by

WILLIAM CARLOS WILLIAMS

with an afterword by the author

Edited and with an introduction
by Jonathan Cohen

A NEW DIRECTIONS PAPERBOOK

Manufactured in the United States of America
New Directions books are printed on acid-free paper
This centennial edition first published as New Directions Paperbook 1389 in 2017

Library of Congress Cataloging-in-Publication Data
Names: Williams, William Carlos, 1883–1963, author. |
Cohen, Jonathan, 1949 May 4– editor.
Title: Al que quiere! : a centennial edition / William Carlos Williams ;
edited and with an introduction by Jonathan Cohen ; afterword and translation
of "The Man Who Resembled a Horse" by William Carlos Williams.
Description: First New Directions paperback edition. |
New York : New Directions Books, 2017.
Identifiers: LCCN 2017018497 | ISBN 9780811226660 (alk. paper)
Classification: LCC PS3545.I544 A6 2017 | DDC 811/.52—dc23
LC record available at https://lccn.loc.gov/2017018497

10 9 8 7 6 5 4 3 2 1

New Directions Books are published for James Laughlin
by New Directions Publishing Corporation
80 Eighth Avenue, New York 10011

Había sido un arbusto desmedrado que prolonga sus filamentos hasta encontrar el humus necesario en una tierra nueva. ¡Y cómo me nutría! Me nutría con la beatitud con que las hojas trémulas de clorofila se extienden al sol; con la beatitud con que una raíz encuentra un cadáver en descomposición; con la beatitud con que los convalecientes dan sus pasos vacilantes en las mañanas de primavera, bañadas de luz;...

RAFAEL ARÉVALO MARTÍNEZ

CONTENTS

THIS VOICE WE CALL WILLIAMS

> *A poem is tough by no quality it borrows from a logical recital of events nor from the events themselves but solely from that attenuated power which draws perhaps many broken things into a dance giving them thus a full being.*
>
> —W. C. Williams, *Kora in Hell*

As William Carlos Williams told Marianne Moore in a letter:

> I want to call my book:
>
> A Book of Poems:
> ### AL QUE QUIERE!
>
> —which means: To him who wants it—but I like the Spanish just as I like a Chinese image cut out of stone: it is decorative and has a certain integral charm. But such a title is not democratic—does not truly represent the contents of the book, so I have added:
>
> A Book of Poems:
> ### AL QUE QUIERE!
> or
> ### THE PLEASURES OF DEMOCRACY.
>
> Now I like this conglomerate title! It is nearly a perfect image of my own grinning mug (seen from the inside), but my publisher objects—and I shake and wobble.

This was in February 1917. When the book was finally published later that year in November, the title was simply *Al Que Quiere!* No "conglomerate" title. It was Williams's third book of poems, but most important, it was his first book to present the voice we call Williams—free verse at once modern and subtly baroque, colloquial, imagistic, distinctly American in its language. No other poet sounded like him.

Al Que Quiere! contains fifty-two poems, the number suggesting not only the number of weeks in the solar year but the number of sections in Walt Whitman's signature poem, "Song of Myself." Several of Williams's poems here are among his most well-known work: "Tract," "Apology," "El Hombre," "Smell!," "Danse Russe," and "January Morning." The poems are set against a background of small town life; that is, Williams's life as family man, physician, and citizen in his hometown Rutherford, New Jersey, across the river from the great metropolis of New York. The long final poem, "The Wanderer," is his early Whitmanesque vision of the poet in a modern industrialized landscape, where "the filthy Passaic" enters the poet's "heart." This poem in its local subject anticipates his epic masterpiece, *Paterson*.

The publisher of the book was Edmund Brown of Boston-based Four Seas Press. Brown was also an early publisher of William Faulkner, Gertrude Stein, and Conrad Aiken, among other notable authors. Brown had good taste, and published a good deal of poetry as well as fiction. He told Williams: "Most of the booksellers are still dead and always will be dead. We are doing our dam[n] best to prod them, however.... I'm still an optimist. There are 110,000,000 people in the United States, and you can sell them 150 copies of a good book of poetry in three years. Now I'm publishing a beauty parlor journal, and expect to make a million." Brown would publish Williams's next two books, *Kora in Hell* (1920) and *Sour Grapes* (1921).

With *Al Que Quiere!* Williams had come a long way from the conventional poetics of his Keatsian *Poems* (1909). In that self-published book which later he preferred to deny ("the poems are obviously young, obviously bad"), he was trying to sound like English Romantic John Keats. As he says in his *Autobiography*: "Keats, during the years at medical school, was my God.... I copied Keats's style religiously, starting my magnum opus of those days on the pattern of *Endymion*." The poems of his second book, *The Tempers* (1913), published in London and with an introductory note by his friend Ezra Pound who had arranged for the book's publication, show Williams maturing and advancing poetically. He was quitting rhyme, for one thing. As he explains in *I Wanted to Write a Poem*: "I was beginning to turn away from the romantic. It may have been my studies in medicine; it may have been my intense feeling of Americanism; anyhow I knew that I wanted reality in my poetry and I began to try to let it speak."

Another modern transformation seen in *Al Que Quiere!* — in all but "The Wanderer" — is Williams's abandonment of the conventional typography used for poetry, where the initial word of each line was capitalized. Not appreciated by readers now is how radical, even shocking, this feature of the layout of his poems was at the time of the book's appearance.

The same year *Al Que Quiere!* came out, T. S. Eliot published his *Prufrock and Other Observations*, the total opposite of Williams. In an essay on "The New Poetry" appearing in the June 1918 issue of *The Future*, Pound greeted both books enthusiastically, while recognizing their differences: "Distinct and as different as possible from the orderly statements of Eliot ... are the poems of Carlos Williams, represented ... in a new book of his own, *Al Que Quiere*, "To Whom It May Concern." If the sinuosities and mental quirks of Misses Moore and [Mina] Loy are difficult to follow I do not know what is to be said for Mr. Williams' ramifications and abruptnesses. I do not pretend to follow all of his volts, jerks, sulks, balks, outblurts and jump-overs; but for all his roughness there remains with me the conviction that there is nothing meaningless in his book, not a

To Whom It May Concern!

THIS book is a collection of poems by William Carlos Williams. You, gentle reader, will probably not like it, because it is brutally powerful and scornfully crude. Fortunately, neither the author nor the publishers care much whether you like it or not. The author has done his work, and if you *do* read the book you will agree that he doesn't give a damn for your opinion. His opinion of you is more important than your opinion of him. And we, the publishers, don't much care whether you buy the book or not. It only costs a dollar, so that we can't make much profit out of it. But we have the satisfaction of offering that which will outweigh, in spite of its eighty small pages, a dozen volumes of pretty lyrics. We have the profound satisfaction of publishing a book in which, we venture to predict, the poets of the future will dig for material as the poets of today dig in Whitman's *Leaves of Grass*.

A BOOK OF POEMS

AL QUE QUIERE!

By WILLIAM CARLOS WILLIAMS

Front of dust jacket, 1917 edition

line.... He is rooted. He is at times almost inarticulate, but he is never dry, never without sap in abundance."

As *Al Que Quiere!* was going to press in the fall of 1917, Pound had encouraged Williams in a letter: "You thank your bloomin gawd you've got enough spanish blood to muddy up your mind, and prevent the current American ideation from going through it like a blighted collander. The thing that saves your work is *opacity*, and dont you forget it. Opacity is NOT an American quality. Fizz, swish, gabble of verbiage, these are echt Amerikanisch [truly American]."

The bold statement printed on the dust jacket of the original 1917 edition of the book (see facing page) was clearly both satiric and prophetic, alluding in its defiant pose to Whitman and his "barbaric yawp." Reviewers latched onto it, how the poetry "is brutally powerful and scornfully crude," and how the author "doesn't give a damn" for the reader's opinion; how the author and publisher "have the profound satisfaction of publishing a book in which, [they] venture to predict, the poets of the future will dig for material as the poets of today dig in Whitman's *Leaves of Grass*." How true, as time would prove! Whitman had since Williams's college days been a model of poetic daring and Americanism, from the subjects of his poems to his use of the language spoken in the United States, not "English" but American, as Williams liked to call it: "the American idiom."

Not surprisingly, the book's critical reception among the literary establishment—what little it received—was mixed. Modernism was still at odds with the conventional. Nineteen seventeen was a big year for Edna St. Vincent Millay and her first book, which by and large critics loved; while a very modern woman, her poetry was formal, rhymed, and metered, using archaic "poetic" diction and phrase inversions. The review of *Al Que Quiere!* published in *Poetry* stated: "As preface to these poems the publishers have been, I think, foolish in dealing the 'gentle reader,' as they are pleased to call him, a kind of blow over the head.... One would expect to find in *Al Que Quiere*, despite its brief number of pages, a veritable *tour de force*, a kind of poetic Woolworth Building, massing magnificently on the horizon, but to the closer eye perhaps inexpressive, harsh, from sheer neglect of detail. One looks in vain, however, for enormous violent shapes, and finds instead poetry of the sparer, more meticulous sort—at its best fibrous, marvelously observant, delicate, haunting; then at moments stilted, confused, obtuse."

An essay in *The Yale Review*, titled "New Poets in a New Age," had this negative take: "A recent book of free verse is recommended to the public by the following publisher's note: 'You, gentle reader, will probably not like it, because it is brutally powerful and scornfully crude.... The author has done his work, and ... doesn't give a damn for your opinion.' Because certain keen minds have revolted against excesses of public prudishness, therefore weaker imitators must serve up the garbage of human thought as mental nourishment. We deplore frankly the reign in poetry of a canting secretiveness; but there is one thing in literature which is worse than conventional morality, and that is conventional immorality. Thanks to the greatness of Whitman ... that is precisely what we are getting to-day." Were Whitman still alive, he surely could sympathize with Williams over such an attack, as, for instance, *The New York Times* said the author of the 1856 edition of *Leaves of Grass* "roots like a pig among a rotten garbage of licentious thoughts."

For Williams, the important reviews came in letters of praise and encouragement written by fellow poets like Moore, Pound, and Wallace Stevens, poets he respected and whose opinions meant a lot to him. Moore told him: "Your compression makes one feel that the Japanese haven't the field to themselves." Her future review of *Kora in Hell* that would appear in *Contact* praised his poetic skills to the hilt: "Compression, color, speed, accuracy and that restraining of instinctive craftsmanship which precludes anything dowdy or labored—it is essentially these qualities that we have in his work." Stevens praised "El Hombre" in particular, using it as the epigraph of one of his own poems, and he told him: "What strikes me most about the poems themselves is their casual character." Noting that "a book of poems is a damned serious affair," he encouraged Williams to carry his "particular quality ... to a communicable extreme, in intensity and volume."

Al Que Quiere! is the culmination of an experimental period of poetry writing that included Williams's translations from Spanish. As he told his brother Edgar in 1910, on returning to the United States after his yearlong pediatrics fellowship in Germany: "I'm going to begin work on a translation from the Spanish in another month. The work is from [Fernando de] Herrera, a lyric poet and a contemporary of Shakespeare's. He has never been done into English but is nevertheless one of the world's masters as Pound assures me.... No kind of practice is better than just such translating work." He included a sequence of anonymous ballads called "Translations from the Spanish" in *The Tempers*. After that, he worked on translating Lope de Vega's Golden Age verse drama, *El nuevo mundo descubierto por Cristóbal Colón* (*The New World Discovered by Christopher Columbus*). His translation is evidently lost, but his praise of Lope's line as "shorter, swifter" than blank verse is on record—"more acceptable to our temperament, manner of thought and speech."

Williams's collaboration with his father, William George Williams, translating the work of several contemporary Latin American poets took place in 1916. Their translations formed the "Spanish-American Number" of *Others*, published in

August of that year. These translations not only functioned as Hispanic personae for Williams—for the "Carlos" in him—they also expanded his experimentation with free verse and lines of varying length shaped by patterns of speech. Beyond that, by using Spanish for the title of his book of poems, Williams would celebrate the "Spanish" (Puerto Rican) part of his identity. It was a dramatic departure from the title he was considering for the book during the summer of 1916, namely, *Pagan Promises*. Four poems in the book have Spanish titles, too.

Al Que Quiere! has an epigraph in Spanish taken from "El hombre que parecía un caballo," a short story by the Guatemalan author Rafael Arévalo Martínez published in 1915. Williams's translation of the story, made with the help of his father, was published in *The Little Review* in 1918 under the title "The Man Who Resembled a Horse." In his translation, the epigraph begins this way: "I had been an adventurous shrub which prolongs its filaments until it finds the necessary humus in new earth. And how I fed!" The spelling errors in the Spanish text due to a careless transcription angered Williams's father, who, though an Englishman, had grown up in the West Indies and was as fluent in Spanish as the poet's Puerto Rican mother (*nueva* was misspelled as "neuva," *beatitud* as "beautitud," and *descomposición* as "descomposition"). Despite these typos, this epigraph pointed smartly to Williams's experience with the new American poetry in both English and Spanish and to other avant-garde arts he encountered in New York leading up to the poems of *Al Que Quiere!* It provides a key to the poetry here.

The present edition includes Williams's translation of the fabulous story in its entirety. Arévalo Martínez published several books of poetry during his lifetime, but is remembered more for his fiction, in particular his "psychozoological" short stories. "The Man Who Resembled a Horse" is deemed his most famous work in this vein. In fact, the story has been called the most famous Latin American short story of the twentieth century. Williams's translations of Arévalo Martínez's poems were the most prominent in the "Spanish-American Number" of *Others*. They can be found in Williams's *By Word of Mouth: Poems from the Spanish, 1916–1959*. Clearly, Arévalo Martínez appealed to Williams on multiple levels at this formative stage in his development as a poet and writer. Both were moving toward a down-to-earth poetic language made of everyday speech.

Williams's poetry is only for those who want it, those willing to give themselves over to its American prosody and its opacity and the images of the world used by the poet. Plus, the baroque wordplay he learned from Spanish Golden Age masters like Luis de Góngora ("the man!"). As he told his mother—the "old woman" addressed in "January Morning"—who had rejected his modernist verse:

> I wanted to write a poem
> that you would understand.
> For what good is it to me
> if you can't understand it?
> 　　　　But you got to try hard—
> But—
> 　　　　Well, you know how
> the young girls run giggling
> on Park Avenue* after dark
> when they ought to be home in bed?
> Well,
> that's the way it is with me somehow.

The purpose of New Directions' centennial edition of *Al Que Quiere!* is to celebrate this voice we call Williams and the real greatness he possesses in his enduring work. To this end, it

---

* In Rutherford, New Jersey. —Ed.

would be helpful to share what he told his audience before a poetry reading he gave at UCLA: "If you don't know what I am talking about ... just remember that I didn't ask you to understand anything, only to listen."

JONATHAN COHEN
NEW YORK 2017

AL QUE QUIERE!

SUB TERRA

Where shall I find you,
you my grotesque fellows
that I seek everywhere
to make up my band?
None, not one
with the earthy tastes I require;
the burrowing pride that rises
subtly as on a bush in May.

Where are you this day,
you my seven year locusts
with cased wings?
Ah my beauties how I long—!
That harvest
that shall be your advent—
thrusting up through the grass,
up under the weeds
answering me,
that shall be satisfying!
The light shall leap and snap
that day as with a million lashes!

Oh, I have you; yes
you are about me in a sense:
playing under the blue pools
that are my windows,—
but they shut you out still,
there in the half light.

For the simple truth is
that though I see you clear enough
you are not there!

It is not that—it is you,
you I want!

—God, if I could fathom
the guts of shadows!

You to come with me
poking into negro houses
with their gloom and smell!
In among children
leaping around a dead dog!
Mimicking
onto the lawns of the rich!
You!
to go with me a-tip-toe,
head down under heaven,
nostrils lipping the wind!

PASTORAL

When I was younger
it was plain to me
I must make something of myself.
Older now
I walk back streets
admiring the houses

of the very poor:
roof out of line with sides
the yards cluttered
with old chicken wire, ashes,
furniture gone wrong;
the fences and outhouses
built of barrel-staves
and parts of boxes, all,
if I am fortunate,
smeared a bluish green
that properly weathered
pleases me best
of all colors.

No one
will believe this
of vast import to the nation.

CHICKORY AND DAISIES

I.

Lift your flowers
on bitter stems
chickory!
Lift them up
out of the scorched ground!
Bear no foliage
but give yourself
wholly to that!

Strain under them
you bitter stems
that no beast eats—
and scorn greyness!
Into the heat with them:
cool!
luxuriant! sky-blue!
The earth cracks and
is shriveled up;
the wind moans piteously;
the sky goes out
if you should fail.

II.

I saw a child with daisies
for weaving into the hair
tear the stems
with her teeth!

METRIC FIGURE

There is a bird in the poplars!
It is the sun!
The leaves are little yellow fish
swimming in the river.
The bird skims above them,
day is on his wings.
Phœbus!
It is he that is making
the great gleam among the poplars!

It is his singing
outshines the noise
of leaves clashing in the wind.

WOMAN WALKING

An oblique cloud of purple smoke
across a milky silhouette
of house sides and tiny trees—
a little village—
that ends in a saw edge
of mist-covered trees
on a sheet of grey sky.

To the right, jutting in,
a dark crimson corner of roof.
To the left, half a tree:

    —what a blessing it is
to see you in the street again,
powerful woman,
coming with swinging haunches,
breasts straight forward,
supple shoulders, full arms
and strong, soft hands (I've felt them)
carrying the heavy basket.
I might well see you oftener!
And for a different reason
than the fresh eggs
you bring us so regularly.

Yes, you, young as I,
with boney brows,
kind grey eyes and a kind mouth;
you walking out toward me
from that dead hillside!
I might well see you oftener.

GULLS

My townspeople, beyond in the great world,
are many with whom it were far more
profitable for me to live than here with you.
These whirr about me calling, calling!
and for my own part I answer them, loud as I can,
but they, being free, pass!
I remain! Therefore, listen!
For you will not soon have another singer.

First I say this: you have seen
the strange birds, have you not, that sometimes
rest upon our river in winter?
Let them cause you to think well then of the storms
that drive many to shelter. These things
do not happen without reason.

And the next thing I say is this:
I saw an eagle once circling against the clouds
over one of our principal churches—
Easter, it was—a beautiful day!—:
three gulls came from above the river
and crossed slowly seaward!

Oh, I know you have your own hymns, I have heard them—
and because I knew they invoked some great protector
I could not be angry with you, no matter
how much they outraged true music—

You see, it is not necessary for us to leap at each other,
and, as I told you, in the end
the gulls moved seaward very quietly.

APPEAL

You who are so mighty,
crimson salamander,
hear me once more.
I lay among the half-burned sticks
at the edge of the fire.
The fiend was creeping in.
I felt the cold tips of fingers—

O crimson salamander!

Give me one little flame,
one!
that I may bind it
protectingly about the wrist
of him that flung me here,
here upon the very center!

This is my song.

IN HARBOR

Surely there, among the great docks, is peace, my mind;
there with the ships moored in the river.
Go out, timid child,
and snuggle in among the great ships talking so quietly.
Maybe you will even fall asleep near them and be
lifted into one of their laps, and in the morning—
There is always the morning in which to remember it all!
Of what are they gossiping? God knows.
And God knows it matters little for we cannot understand them.
Yet it is certainly of the sea, of that there can be no question.
It is a quiet sound. Rest! That's all I care for now.
The smell of them will put us to sleep presently.
Smell! It is the sea water mingling here into the river—
at least so it seems—perhaps it is something else—but what matter?

◆

The sea water! It is quiet and smooth here!
How slowly they move, little by little trying
the hawsers that drop and groan with their agony.
Yes, it is certainly of the high sea they are talking.

WINTER SUNSET

Then I raised my head
and stared out over
the blue February waste
to the blue bank of hill
with stars on it
in strings and festoons—

but above that:
one opaque
stone of a cloud
just on the hill
left and right
as far as I could see;
and above that
a red streak, then
icy blue sky!

It was a fearful thing
to come into a man's heart
at that time: that stone
over the little blinking stars
they'd set there.

APOLOGY

Why do I write today?

The beauty of
the terrible faces
of our nonentities
stirs me to it:

colored women
day workers—
old and experienced—
returning home at dusk
in cast off clothing

faces like
old Florentine oak.

Also

the set pieces
of your faces stir me—
leading citizens—
but not
in the same way.

PASTORAL

The little sparrows
hop ingenuously
about the pavement
quarreling
with sharp voices
over those things
that interest them.
But we who are wiser
shut ourselves in
on either hand
and no one knows
whether we think good
or evil.
            Meanwhile,
the old man who goes about
gathering dog-lime
walks in the gutter

without looking up
and his tread
is more majestic than
that of the Episcopal minister
approaching the pulpit
of a Sunday.
              These things
astonish me beyond words.

LOVE SONG

Daisies are broken
petals are news of the day
stems lift to the grass tops
they catch on shoes
part in the middle
leave root and leaves secure.

Black branches
carry square leaves
to the wood's top.
They hold firm
break with a roar
show the white!

Your moods are slow
the shedding of leaves
and sure
the return in May!

We walked
in your father's grove
and saw the great oaks
lying with roots
ripped from the ground.

M. B.

Winter has spent this snow
out of envy, but spring is here!
He sits at the breakfast table
in his yellow hair
and disdains even the sun
walking outside
in spangled slippers:

He looks out: there is
a glare of lights
before a theater,—
a sparkling lady
passes quickly to
the seclusion of
her carriage.
    Presently
under the dirty, wavy heaven
of a borrowed room he will make
re-inhaled tobacco smoke
his clouds and try them
against the sky's limits!

TRACT

I will teach you   my townspeople
how to perform   a funeral—
for you have it   over a troop
of artists—
unless one should   scour the world—
you have the ground sense   necessary.

See!   the hearse leads.
I begin with   a design for a hearse.
For Christ's sake   not black—
nor white either—   and not polished!
Let it be weathered—   like a farm wagon—
with gilt wheels   (this could be
applied fresh   at small expense)
or no wheels at all:
a rough dray to   drag over the ground.

Knock the glass out!
My God—glass,   my townspeople!
For what purpose?   Is it for the dead
to look out or   for us to see
how well he is housed   or to see
the flowers or   the lack of them—
or what?
To keep the rain   and snow from him?
He will have a   heavier rain soon:
pebbles and dirt   and what not.
Let there be no glass—
and no upholstery   phew!

The caesuras indicated by extra space mirror the line breaks in the poem's
first publication in *Others* (Feb. 1916). —Ed.

and no little   brass rollers
and small easy wheels   on the bottom—
my townspeople   what are you thinking of?

A rough   plain hearse then
with gilt wheels   and no top at all.
On this   the coffin lies
by its own weight.

          No wreathes please—
especially no   hot house flowers.
Some common memento   is better,
something he prized   and is known by:
his old clothes—   a few books perhaps—
God knows what!   You realize
how we are   about these things
my townspeople—
something will be found—   anything
even flowers   if he had come to that.

So much for   the hearse.
For heaven's sake though   see to the driver!
Take off   the silk hat! In fact
that's no place   at all for him—
up there   unceremoniously
dragging our friend out   to his own dignity!
Bring him down—   bring him down!
Low and inconspicuous!   I'd not have him ride
on the wagon at all—   damn him—
the undertaker's   understrapper!
Let him hold   the reins
and walk   at the side
and inconspicuously   too!

Then briefly   as to yourselves:
Walk behind—   as they do in France,
seventh class, or   if you ride
Hell take curtains!   Go with some show
of inconvenience;   sit openly—
to the weather   as to grief.
Or do you think   you can shut grief in?
What—from us?   We who have perhaps
nothing to lose?   Share with us
share with us—   it will be money
in your pockets.
                Go now
I think you are   ready.

PROMENADE

I.

Well, mind, here we have
our little son beside us:
a little diversion before breakfast!

Come, we'll walk down the road
till the bacon will be frying.
We might better be idle?
A poem might come of it?
Oh, be useful. Save annoyance
to Flossie and besides—the wind!
It's cold. It blows our
old pants out! It makes us shiver!
See the heavy trees
shifting their weight before it.

Let us be trees, an old house,
a hill with grass on it!
The baby's arms are blue.
Come, move! Be quieted!

II.

So. We'll sit here now
and throw pebbles into
this water-trickle.

Splash the water up!
(Splash it up, Sonny!) Laugh!
Hit it there deep under the grass.
See it splash! Ah, mind,
see it splash! It is alive!
Throw pieces of broken leaves
into it. They'll pass through.
No! Yes—just!

Away now for the cows! But—
It's cold!
It's getting dark.
It's going to rain.
No further!

III.

Oh then, a wreath! Let's
refresh something they
used to write well of.

Two fern plumes. Strip them
to the mid-rib along one side.
Bind the tips with a grass stem.
Bend and intertwist the stalks
at the back. So!
Ah! now we are crowned!
Now we are a poet!

Quickly!
A bunch of little flowers
for Flossie—the little ones
only:
            a red clover, one
blue heal-all, a sprig of
bone-set, one primrose,
a head of Indian tobacco, this
magenta speck and this
little lavender!
                  Home now, my mind!—
Sonny's arms are icy, I tell you—
and have breakfast!

EL HOMBRE

It's a strange courage
you give me ancient star:

Shine alone in the sunrise
toward which you lend no part!

HERO

Fool,
put your adventures
into those things
which break ships—
not female flesh.

Let there pass
over the mind
the waters of
four oceans, the airs
of four skies!

Return hollow-bellied,
keen-eyed, hard!
A simple scar or two.

Little girls will come
bringing you
roses for your button-hole.

LIBERTAD! IGUALDAD! FRATERNIDAD!

You sullen pig of a man
you force me into the mud
with your stinking ash-cart!

Brother!
            —if we were rich
we'd stick our chests out
and hold our heads high!

It is dreams that have destroyed us.

There is no more pride
in horses or in rein holding.
We sit hunched together brooding
our fate.

            Well—
all things turn bitter in the end
whether you choose the right or
the left way
            and—
dreams are not a bad thing.

CANTHARA

The old black-man showed me
how he had been shocked
in his youth
by six women, dancing
a set-dance, stark naked below
the skirts raised round
their breasts:

                    bellies flung forward
knees flying!
                        —while
his gestures, against the
tiled wall of the dingy bath-room,
swished with ecstasy to
the familiar music of
                        his old emotion.

MUJER

Oh, black Persian cat!
Was not your life
already cursed with offspring?
We took you for rest to that old
Yankee farm,—so lonely
and with so many field mice
in the long grass—
and you return to us
in this condition—!

Oh, black Persian cat.

SUMMER SONG

Wanderer moon
smiling a
faintly ironical smile
at this
brilliant, dew-moistened

summer morning,—
a detached
sleepily indifferent
smile, a
wanderer's smile,—
if I should
buy a shirt
your color and
put on a necktie
sky blue
where would they carry me?

LOVE SONG

Sweep the house clean,
hang fresh curtains
in the windows
put on a new dress
and come with me!
The elm is scattering
its little loaves
of sweet smells
from a white sky!

Who shall hear of us
in the time to come?
Let him say there was
a burst of fragrance
from black branches.

FOREIGN

Artsybashev is a Russian.
I am an American.
Let us wonder, my townspeople,
if Artsybashev tends his own fires
as I do, gets himself cursed
for the baby's failure to thrive,
loosens windows for the woman
who cleans his parlor—
or has he neat servants
and a quiet library, an
intellectual wife perhaps and
no children,—an apartment
somewhere in a back street or
lives alone or with his mother
or sister—

I wonder, my townspeople,
if Artsybashev looks upon
himself the more concernedly
or succeeds any better than I
in laying the world.

I wonder which is the bigger
fool in his own mind.

These are shining topics
my townspeople but—
hardly of great moment.

A PRELUDE

I know only the bare rocks of today.
In these lies my brown sea-weed,—
green quartz veins bent through the wet shale;
in these lie my pools left by the tide—
quiet, forgetting waves;
on these stiffen white star fish;
on these I slip bare footed!

Whispers of the fishy air touch my body;
"Sisters," I say to them.

HISTORY

I.

A wind might blow a lotus petal
over the pyramids—but not this wind.

Summer is a dried leaf.

Leaves stir this way then that
on the baked asphalt, the wheels
of motor cars rush over them,—
     gas smells mingle with leaf smells.

Oh, Sunday, day of worship! ! !

The steps to the museum are high.
Worshippers pass in and out.

Nobody comes here today.
I come here to mingle faience dug
from the tomb, turquoise colored
necklaces and belched wind from the
stomach; delicately veined basins
of agate, cracked and discolored and
the stink of stale urine!

Enter! Elbow in at the door.
Men? Women?
Simpering, clay fetish-faces counting
through the turnstile.
                    Ah!

                    II.

This sarcophagus contained the body
of Uresh-Nai, priestess to the goddess Mut,
Mother of All—

Run your finger against this edge!
—here went the chisel!—and think
of an arrogance endured six thousand years
without a flaw!

But love is an oil to embalm the body.
Love is a packet of spices, a strong-
smelling liquid to be squirted into
the thigh. No?
Love rubbed on a bald head will make
hair—and after? Love is
a lice comber!
                    Gnats on dung!

"The chisel is in your hand, the block
is before you, cut as I shall dictate:
this is the coffin of Uresh-Nai,
priestess to the sky goddess,—built
to endure forever!
                            Carve the inside
with the image of my death in
little lines of figures three fingers high.
Put a lid on it cut with Mut bending over
the earth, for my headpiece, and in the year
to be chosen I will rouse, the lid
shall be lifted and I will walk about
the temple where they have rested me
and eat the air of the place:

Ah—these walls are high! This
is in keeping."

III.

The priestess has passed into her tomb.
The stone has taken up her spirit!
Granite over flesh: who will deny
its advantages?

Your death?—water
spilled upon the ground—
though water will mount again into rose-leaves—
but you?—would hold life still,
even as a memory, when it is over.
Benevolence is rare.

Climb about this sarcophagus, read
what is writ for you in these figures,
hard as the granite that has held them
with so soft a hand the while
your own flesh has been fifty times
through the guts of oxen,—read!
"The rose-tree will have its donor
even though he give stingily.
The gift of some endures
ten years, the gift of some twenty
and the gift of some for the time a
great house rots and is torn down.
Some give for a thousand years to men of
one face, some for a thousand
to all men and some few to all men
while granite holds an edge against
the weather.
              Judge then of love!"

                    IV.

"My flesh is turned to stone. I
have endured my summer. The flurry
of falling petals is ended. Lay
the finger upon this granite. I was
well desired and fully caressed
by many lovers but my flesh
withered swiftly and my heart was
never satisfied. Lay your hands
upon the granite as a lover lays his
hand upon the thigh and upon the
round breasts of her who is

beside him, for now I will not wither,
now I have thrown off secrecy, now
I have walked naked into the street,
now I have scattered my heavy beauty
in the open market.
Here I am with head high and a
burning heart eagerly awaiting
your caresses, whoever it may be,
for granite is not harder than
my love is open, runs loose among you!

I arrogant against death! I
who have endured! I worn against
the years!"

v.

But it is five o'clock. Come!
Life is good—enjoy it!
A walk in the park while the day lasts.
I will go with you. Look! this
northern scenery is not the Nile, but—
these benches—the yellow and purple dusk—
the moon there—these tired people—
the lights on the water!

Are not these Jews and—Ethiopians?
The world is young, surely! Young
and colored like—a girl that has come upon
a lover! Will that do?

WINTER QUIET

Limb to limb, mouth to mouth
with the bleached grass
silver mist lies upon the back yards
among the outhouses.
                              The dwarf trees
pirouette awkwardly to it—
whirling round on one toe;
the big tree smiles and glances
                                        upward!
Tense with suppressed excitement
the fences watch where the ground
has humped an aching shoulder for
                              the ecstasy.

DAWN

Ecstatic bird songs pound
the hollow vastness of the sky
with metallic clinkings—
beating color up into it
at a far edge,—beating it, beating it
with rising, triumphant ardor,—
stirring it into warmth,
quickening in it a spreading change,—
bursting wildly against it as
dividing the horizon, a heavy sun
lifts himself—is lifted—
bit by bit above the edge
of things,—runs free at last
out into the open—! lumbering

glorified in full release upward—

                                songs cease.

GOOD NIGHT

In brilliant gas light
I turn the kitchen spigot
and watch the water plash
into the clean white sink.
On the grooved drain-board
to one side is
a glass filled with parsley—
crisped green.

                    Waiting
for the water to freshen—
I glance at the spotless floor—:
a pair of rubber sandals
lie side by side
under the wall-table,
all is in order for the night.

Waiting, with a glass in my hand
—three girls in crimson satin
pass close before me on
the murmurous background of
the crowded opera—

                        it is
memory playing the clown—
three vague, meaningless girls
full of smells and
the rustling sound of
cloth rubbing on cloth and

little slippers on carpet—
high-school French
spoken in a loud voice!

Parsley in a glass,
still and shining,
brings me back. I take my drink
and yawn deliciously.
I am ready for bed.

DANSE RUSSE

If I when my wife is sleeping
and the baby and Kathleen
are sleeping
and the sun is a flame-white disc
in silken mists
above shining trees,—
if I in my north room
danse naked, grotesquely
before my mirror
waving my shirt round my head
and singing softly to myself:
"I am lonely, lonely.
I was born to be lonely.
I am best so!"
If I admire my arms, my face
my shoulders, flanks, buttocks
against the yellow drawn shades,—

who shall say I am not
the happy genius of my household?

PORTRAIT OF A WOMAN IN BED

There's my things
drying in the corner:
that blue skirt
joined to the grey shirt—

I'm sick of trouble!
Lift the covers
if you want me
and you'll see
the rest of my clothes—
though it would be cold
lying with nothing on!

I won't work
and I've got no cash.
What are you going to do
about it?
—and no jewelry
(the crazy fools)

But I've my two eyes
and a smooth face
and here's this! look!
it's high!
There's brains and blood
in there—
my name's Robitza!
Corsets
can go to the devil—
and drawers along with them!
What do I care!

My two boys?
—they're keen!
Let the rich lady
care for them—
they'll beat the school
or
let them go to the gutter—
that ends trouble.

This house is empty
isn't it?
Then it's mine
because I need it.
Oh, I won't starve
while there's the Bible
to make them feed me.

Try to help me
if you want trouble
or leave me alone—
that ends trouble.

The county physician
is a damned fool
and you
can go to hell!

You could have closed the door
when you came in;
do it when you go out.
I'm tired.

VIRTUE

Now? Why—
whirl-pools of
orange and purple flame
feather twists of chrome
on a green ground
funneling down upon
the steaming phallus-head
of the mad sun himself—
blackened crimson!

                    Now?

Why—
it is the smile of her
the smell of her
the vulgar inviting mouth of her!
It is—Oh, nothing new
nothing that lasts
an eternity, nothing worth
putting out to interest,
nothing—
but the fixing of an eye
concretely upon emptiness!

Come! here are—
cross-eyed men, a boy
with a patch, men walking
in their shirts, men in hats
dark men, a pale man
with little black moustaches
and a dirty white coat,

fat men with pudgy faces,
thin faces, crooked faces
slit eyes, grey eyes, black eyes
old men with dirty beards,
men in vests with
gold watch chains. Come!

CONQUEST

[*Dedicated to F. W.*]

Hard, chilly colors:
straw grey, frost grey
the grey of frozen ground:
and you, O sun,
close above the horizon!
It is I holds you—
half against the sky
half against a black tree trunk
icily resplendent!

Lie there, blue city, mine at last—
rimming the banked blue grey
and rise, indescribable smoky yellow
into the overpowering white!

PORTRAIT OF A YOUNG MAN
WITH A BAD HEART

Have I seen her?
Only through the window
across the street.

If I go meeting her
on the corner
some damned fool
will go blabbing it
to the old man and
she'll get hell.
He's a queer old bastard!
Every time he sees me
you'd think
I wanted to kill him.
But I figure it out
it's best to let things
stay as they are—
for a while at least.

It's hard
giving up the thing
you want most
in the world, but with this
damned pump of mine
liable to give out …

She's a good kid
and I'd hate to hurt her
but if she can get over it—

it'd be the best thing.

KELLER GEGEN DOM

Witness, would you—
one more young man
in the evening of his love
hurrying to confession:
steps down a gutter
crosses a street
goes in at a doorway
opens for you—
like some great flower—
a room filled with lamplight;
or whirls himself
obediently to
the curl of a hill
some wind-dancing afternoon;
lies for you in
the futile darkness of
a wall, sets stars dancing
to the crack of a leaf—

and—leaning his head away—
snuffs (secretly)
the bitter powder from

his thumb's hollow,
takes your blessing and
goes home to bed?

Witness instead
whether you like it or not
a dark vinegar smelling place
from which trickles
the chuckle of
beginning laughter.

It strikes midnight.

SMELL!

Oh strong ridged and deeply hollowed
nose of mine! what will you not be smelling?
What tactless asses we are, you and I, boney nose,
always indiscriminate, always unashamed,
and now it is the souring flowers of the bedraggled
poplars: a festering pulp on the wet earth
beneath them. With what deep thirst
we quicken our desires
to that rank odor of a passing spring-time!
Can you not be decent? Can you not reserve your ardors
for something less unlovely? What girl will care
for us, do you think, if we continue in these ways?
Must you taste everything? Must you know everything?
Must you have a part in everything?

BALLET

Are you not weary,
great gold cross
shining in the wind—
are you not weary
of seeing the stars
turning over you
and the sun
going to his rest
and you frozen with
a great lie
that leaves you
rigid as a knight
on a marble coffin?

—and you,
higher, still,
          robin,
untwisting a song
from the bare
top-twigs,
are you not
weary of labor,
even the labor of
a song?

Come down—join me
for I am lonely.

First it will be
a quiet pace
to ease our stiffness
but as the west yellows
you will be ready!
Here in the middle
of the roadway
we will fling
ourselves round
with dust lilies
till we are bound in
their twining stems!
We will tear
their flowers
with arms flashing!

And when
the astonished stars
push aside
their curtains
they will see us
fall exhausted where
wheels and
the pounding feet
of horses
will crush forth
our laughter.

SYMPATHETIC PORTRAIT OF A CHILD

The murderer's little daughter
who is barely ten years old
jerks her shoulders
right and left
so as to catch a glimpse of me
without turning round.

Her skinny little arms
wrap themselves
this way then that
reversely about her body!
Nervously
she crushes her straw hat
about her eyes
and tilts her head
to deepen the shadow—
smiling excitedly!

As best as she can
she hides herself
in the full sunlight
her cordy legs writhing
beneath the little flowered dress
that leaves them bare
from mid-thigh to ankle—

Why has she chosen me
for the knife
that darts along her smile?

THE OGRE

Sweet child,
little girl with well shaped legs
you cannot touch the thoughts
I put over and under and around you.
This is fortunate for they would
burn you to an ash otherwise.
Your petals would be quite curled up.

This is all beyond you—no doubt,
yet you do feel the brushings
of the fine needles;
the tentative lines of your whole body
prove it to me;
so does your fear of me,
your shyness;
likewise the toy baby cart
that you are pushing—
and besides, mother has begun
to dress your hair in a knot.
These are my excuses.

RIPOSTE

Love is like water or the air
my townspeople;
it cleanses, and dissipates evil gases.
It is like poetry too
and for the same reasons.

Love is so precious
my townspeople
that if I were you I would
have it under lock and key—
like the air or the Atlantic or
like poetry!

THE OLD MEN

Old men who have studied
every leg show
in the city
Old men cut from touch
by the perfumed music—
polished or fleeced skulls
that stand before
the whole theater
in silent attitudes
of attention,—
old men who have taken precedence
over young men
and even over dark-faced
husbands whose minds
are a street with arc-lights.
Solitary old men for whom
we find no excuses—
I bow my head in shame
for those who malign you.
Old men

the peaceful beer of impotence
be yours!

PASTORAL

If I say I have heard voices
who will believe me?

>"None has dipped his hand
>in the black waters of the sky
>nor picked the yellow lilies
>that sway on their clear stems
>and no tree has waited
>long enough nor still enough
>to touch fingers with the moon."

I looked and there were little frogs
with puffed out throats,
singing in the slime.

SPRING STRAINS

In a tissue-thin monotone of blue-grey buds
crowded erect with desire against
the sky—
          tense blue-grey twigs
slenderly anchoring them down, drawing
them in—
          two blue-grey birds chasing
a third struggle in circles, angles,

swift convergings to a point that bursts
instantly!
    Vibrant bowing limbs
pull downward, sucking in the sky
that bulges from behind, plastering itself
against them in packed rifts, rock blue
and dirty orange!
    But—
(Hold hard, rigid jointed trees!)
the blinding and red-edged sun-blur—
creeping energy, concentrated
counterforce—welds sky, buds, trees,
rivets them in one puckering hold!
Sticks through! Pulls the whole
counter-pulling mass upward, to the right,
locks even the opaque, not yet defined
ground in a terrific drag that is
loosening the very tap-roots!

On a tissue-thin monotone of blue-grey buds
two blue-grey birds, chasing a third,
at full cry! Now they are
flung outward and up—disappearing suddenly!

TREES

Crooked, black tree
on your little grey-black hillock,
ridiculously raised one step toward
the infinite summits of the night:
even you the few grey stars

46

draw upward into a vague melody
of harsh threads.

Bent as you are from straining
against the bitter horizontals of
a north wind,—there below you
how easily the long yellow notes
of poplars flow upward in a descending
scale, each note secure in its own
posture—singularly woven.

All voices are blent willingly
against the heaving contra-bass
of the dark but you alone
warp yourself passionately to one side
in your eagerness.

A PORTRAIT IN GREYS

Will it never be possible
to separate you from your greyness?
Must you be always sinking backward
into your grey-brown landscapes—and trees
always in the distance, always against
a grey sky?
                    Must I be always
moving counter to you? Is there no place
where we can be at peace together
and the motion of our drawing apart
be altogether taken up?
                              I see myself

standing upon your shoulders touching
a grey, broken sky—
but you, weighted down with me,
yet gripping my ankles,—move
                            laboriously on,
where it is level and undisturbed by colors.

INVITATION

You who had the sense
to choose me such a mother,
you who had the indifference
to create me,
you who went to some pains
to leave hands off me
in the formative stages,—
(I thank you most for that
perhaps)
                            but you who
with an iron head, first,
fiercest and with strongest love
brutalized me into strength,
old dew-lap,—
I have reached the stage
where I am teaching myself
to laugh.
                            Come on,
take a walk with me.

DIVERTIMIENTO

Miserable little woman
in a brown coat—

                quit whining!
My hand for you!
We'll skip down the tin cornices
of Main Street
flicking the dull roof-line
with our toe-tips!
Hop clear of the bank! A
pin-wheel round the white flag-pole.

And I'll sing you the while
a thing to split your sides
about Johann Sebastian Bach,
the father of music, who had
three wives and twenty-two children.

JANUARY MORNING

Suite

                I.

I have discovered that most of
the beauties of travel are due to
the strange hours we keep to see them:

the domes of the Church of
the Paulist Fathers in Weehawken

against a smoky dawn—the heart stirred—
are beautiful as Saint Peters
approached after years of anticipation.

II.

Though the operation was postponed
I saw the tall probationers
in their tan uniforms
                hurrying to breakfast!

III.

—and from basement entrys
neatly coiffed, middle aged gentlemen
with orderly moustaches and
well brushed coats

IV.

—and the sun, dipping into the avenues
streaking the tops of
the irregular red houselets,
                      and
the gay shadows dropping and dropping.

V.

—and a young horse with a green bed-quilt
on his withers shaking his head:
bared teeth and nozzle high in the air!

VI.

—and a semicircle of dirt colored men
about a fire bursting from an old
ash can,

VII.

                —and the worn,
blue car rails (like the sky!)
gleaming among the cobbles!

VIII.

—and the rickety ferry-boat "Arden"!
What an object to be called "Arden"
among the great piers,—on the
ever new river!
                "Put me a Touchstone
at the wheel, white gulls, and we'll
follow the ghost of the *Half Moon*
to the North West Passage—and through!
(at Albany!) for all that!"

IX.

Exquisite brown waves—long
circlets of silver moving over you!
enough with crumbling ice-crusts among you!
The sky has come down to you,
lighter than tiny bubbles, face to
face with you!
                His spirit is
a white gull with delicate pink feet
and a snowy breast for you to
hold to your lips delicately!

X.

The young doctor is dancing with happiness
in the sparkling wind, alone

at the prow of the ferry! He notices
the curdy barnacles and broken ice crusts
left at the slip's base by the low tide
and thinks of summer and green
shell crusted ledges among
                    the emerald eel-grass!

XI.

Who knows the Palisades as I do
knows the river breaks east from them
above the city—but they continue south
—under the sky—to bear a crest of
little peering houses that brighten
with dawn behind the moody
water-loving giants of Manhattan.

XII.

Long yellow rushes bending
above the white snow patches;
purple and gold ribbon
of the distant wood:
                    what an angle
you make with each other as
you lie there in contemplation.

XIII.

Work hard all your young days
and they'll find you too, some morning
staring up under
your chiffonier at its warped
bass-wood bottom and your soul—
out!

—among the little sparrows
behind the shutter.

xiv.

—and the flapping flags are at
half mast for the dead admiral.

xv.

All this—
       was for you, old woman.
I wanted to write a poem
that you would understand.
For what good is it to me
if you can't understand it?
           But you got to try hard—
But—
       Well, you know how
the young girls run giggling
on Park Avenue after dark
when they ought to be home in bed?
Well,
that's the way it is with me somehow.

TO A SOLITARY DISCIPLE

Rather notice, mon cher,
that the moon is
tilted above
the point of the steeple
than that its color
is shell-pink.

Rather observe
that it is early morning
than that the sky
is smooth
as a turquoise.

Rather grasp
how the dark
converging lines
of the steeple
meet at the pinnacle—
perceive how
its little ornament
tries to stop them—

See how it fails!
See how the converging lines
of the hexagonal spire
escape upward—
receding, dividing!
—sepals
that guard and contain
the flower!

Observe
how motionless
the eaten moon
lies in the protecting lines.

It is true:
in the light colors

of morning
brown-stone and slate
shine orange and dark blue.

But observe
the oppressive weight
of the squat edifice!
Observe
the jasmine lightness
of the moon.

DEDICATION FOR A PLOT OF GROUND

This plot of ground
facing the waters of this inlet
is dedicated to the living presence of
Emily Richardson Wellcome
who was born in England; married;
lost her husband and with
her five year old son
sailed for New York in a two-master;
was driven to the Azores;
ran adrift on Fire Island shoal,
met her second husband
in a Brooklyn boarding house,
went with him to Puerto Rico
bore three more children, lost
her second husband, lived hard
for eight years in St. Thomas,
Puerto Rico, San Domingo, followed

the oldest son to New York,
lost her daughter, lost her "baby,"
seized the two boys of
the oldest son by the second marriage
mothered them—they being
motherless—fought for them
against the other grandmother
and the aunts, brought them here
summer after summer, defended
herself here against thieves,
storms, sun, fire,
against flies, against girls
that came smelling about, against
drought, against weeds, storm-tides,
neighbors, weasels that stole her chickens,
against the weakness of her own hands,
against the growing strength of
the boys, against wind, against
the stones, against trespassers,
against rents, against her own mind.

She grubbed this earth with her own hands,
domineered over this grass plot,
blackguarded her oldest son
into buying it, lived here fifteen years,
attained a final loneliness and—

If you can bring nothing to this place
but your carcass, keep out.

K. McB.

You exquisite chunk of mud
Kathleen—just like
any other chunk of mud!
—especially in April!
Curl up round their shoes
when they try to step on you,
spoil the polish!
I shall laugh till I am sick
at their amazement.
Do they expect the ground to be
always solid?
Give them the slip then;
let them sit in you;
soil their pants;
teach them a dignity
that is dignity, the dignity
of mud!

       Lie basking in
the sun then—fast asleep!
Even become dust on occasion.

LOVE SONG

I lie here thinking of you:—

the stain of love
is upon the world!
Yellow, yellow, yellow
it eats into the leaves,
smears with saffron
the horned branches that lean
heavily
against a smooth purple sky!
There is no light
only a honey-thick stain
that drips from leaf to leaf
and limb to limb
spoiling the colors
of the whole world—

you far off there under
the wine-red selvage of the west!

THE WANDERER

A Rococo Study

ADVENT

Even in the time when as yet
I had no certain knowledge of her
She sprang from the nest, a young crow,
Whose first flight circled the forest.
I know now how then she showed me
Her mind, reaching out to the horizon,
She close above the tree tops.
I saw her eyes straining at the new distance
And as the woods fell from her flying
Likewise they fell from me as I followed—
So that I strongly guessed all that I must put from me
To come through ready for the high courses.

But one day, crossing the ferry
With the great towers of Manhattan before me,
Out at the prow with the sea wind blowing,
I had been wearying many questions
Which she had put on to try me:
How shall I be a mirror to this modernity?
When lo! in a rush, dragging
A blunt boat on the yielding river—
Suddenly I saw her! And she waved me
From the white wet in midst of her playing!
She cried me, "Haia! Here I am, son!
See how strong my little finger is!
Can I not swim well?
I can fly too!" And with that a great sea-gull

Went to the left, vanishing with a wild cry—
But in my mind all the persons of godhead
Followed after.

CLARITY

"Come!" cried my mind and by her might
That was upon us we flew above the river
Seeking her, grey gulls among the white—
In the air speaking as she had willed it:
"I am given," cried I, "now I know it!
I know now all my time is forespent!
For me one face is all the world!
For I have seen her at last, this day,
In whom age in age is united—
Indifferent, out of sequence, marvelously!
Saving alone that one sequence
Which is the beauty of all the world, for surely
Either there in the rolling smoke spheres below us
Or here with us in the air intercircling,
Certainly somewhere here about us
I know she is revealing these things!"

And as gulls we flew and with soft cries
We seemed to speak, flying, "It is she
The mighty, recreating the whole world,
This the first day of wonders!
She is attiring herself before me—
Taking shape before me for worship,
A red leaf that falls upon a stone!
It is she of whom I told you, old
Forgiveless, unreconcilable;

That high wanderer of by-ways
Walking imperious in beggary!
At her throat is loose gold, a single chain
From among many, on her bent fingers
Are rings from which the stones are fallen,
Her wrists wear a diminished state, her ankles
Are bare! Toward the river! Is it she there?"
And we swerved clamorously downward—
"I will take my peace in her henceforth!"

BROADWAY

It was then she struck—from behind,
In mid air, as with the edge of a great wing!
And instantly down the mists of my eyes
There came crowds walking—men as visions
With expressionless, animate faces;
Empty men with shell-thin bodies
Jostling close above the gutter,
Hasting—nowhere! And then for the first time
I really saw her, really scented the sweat
Of her presence and—fell back sickened!
Ominous, old, painted—
With bright lips, and lewd Jew's eyes
Her might strapped in by a corset
To give her age youth, perfect
In her will to be young she had covered
The godhead to go beside me.
Silent, her voice entered at my eyes
And my astonished thought followed her easily:
"Well, do their eyes shine, do their clothes fit?
These *live* I tell you! Old men with red cheeks,

Young men in gay suits! See them!
Dogged, quivering, impassive—
Well—are these the ones you envied?"
At which I answered her, "Marvelous old queen,
Grant me power to catch something of this day's
Air and sun into your service!
That these toilers after peace and after pleasure
May turn to you, worshippers at all hours!"
But she sniffed upon the words warily—
Yet I persisted, watching for an answer:
"To you, horrible old woman,
Who know all fires out of the bodies
Of all men that walk with lust at heart!
To you, O mighty, crafty prowler
After the youth of all cities, drunk
With the sight of thy archness! All the youth
That come to you, you having the knowledge
Rather than to those uninitiate—
To you, marvelous old queen, give me always
A new marriage—"
                              But she laughed loudly—
"A new grip upon those garments that brushed me
In days gone by on beach, lawn, and in forest!
May I be lifted still, up and out of terror,
Up from before the death living around me—
Torn up continually and carried
Whatever way the head of your whim is,
A burr upon those streaming tatters—"
But the night had fallen, she stilled me
And led me away.

At the first peep of dawn she roused me!
I rose trembling at the change which the night saw!
For there, wretchedly brooding in a corner
From which her old eyes glittered fiercely—
"Go!" she said, and I hurried shivering
Out into the deserted streets of Paterson.

That night she came again, hovering
In rags within the filmy ceiling—
"Great Queen, bless me with thy tatters!"
"You are blest, go on!"
                              "Hot for savagery,
Sucking the air! I went into the city,
Out again, baffled onto the mountain!
Back into the city!
                    Nowhere
The subtle! Everywhere the electric!"

"A short bread-line before a hitherto empty tea shop:
No questions—all stood patiently,
Dominated by one idea: something
That carried them as they are always wanting to be carried,
'But what is it,' I asked those nearest me,
'This thing heretofore unobtainable
That they seem so clever to have put on now!'

"Why since I have failed them can it be anything but their own
    brood?
Can it be anything but brutality?

On that at least they're united! That at least
Is their bean soup, their calm bread and a few luxuries!

"But in me, more sensitive, marvelous old queen
It sank deep into the blood, that I rose upon
The tense air enjoying the dusty fight!
Heavy drink were the low, sloping foreheads
The flat skulls with the unkempt black or blond hair,
The ugly legs of the young girls, pistons
Too powerful for delicacy!
The women's wrists, the men's arms, red
Used to heat and cold, to toss quartered beeves
And barrels, and milk-cans, and crates of fruit!

"Faces all knotted up like burls on oaks,
Grasping, fox-snouted, thick-lipped,
Sagging breasts and protruding stomachs,
Rasping voices, filthy habits with the hands.

"Nowhere you! Everywhere the electric!

"Ugly, venomous, gigantic!
Tossing me as a great father his helpless
Infant till it shriek with ecstasy
And its eyes roll and its tongue hangs out!—

"I am at peace again, old queen, I listen clearer now."

ABROAD

Never, even in a dream,
Have I winged so high nor so well

64

As with her, she leading me by the hand,
That first day on the Jersey mountains!
And never shall I forget
The trembling interest with which I heard
Her voice in a low thunder:
"You are safe here. Look child, look open-mouth!
The patch of road between the steep bramble banks;
The tree in the wind, the white house there, the sky!
Speak to men of these, concerning me!
For never while you permit them to ignore me
In these shall the full of my freed voice
Come grappling the ear with intent!
Never while the air's clear coolness
Is seized to be a coat for pettiness;
Never while richness of greenery
Stands a shield for prurient minds;
Never, permitting these things unchallenged
Shall my voice of leaves and varicolored bark come free through!"
At which, knowing her solitude,
I shouted over the country below me:
"Waken! my people, to the boughs green
With ripening fruit within you!
Waken to the myriad cinquefoil
In the waving grass of your minds!
Waken to the silent phoebe nest
Under the eaves of your spirit!"

But she, stooping nearer the shifting hills
Spoke again. "Look there! See them!
There in the oat field with the horses,
See them there! bowed by their passions
Crushed down, that had been raised as a roof beam!

The weight of the sky is upon them
Under which all roof beams crumble.
There is none but the single roof beam:
There is no love bears against the great firefly!
At this I looked up at the sun
Then shouted again with all the might I had.
But my voice was a seed in the wind.
Then she, the old one, laughing
Seized me and whirling about bore back
To the city, upward, still laughing
Until the great towers stood above the marshland
Wheeling beneath: the little creeks, the mallows
That I picked as a boy, the Hackensack
So quiet that seemed so broad formerly:
The crawling trains, the cedar swamp on the one side—
All so old, so familiar—so new now
To my marvelling eyes as we passed
Invisible.

SOOTHSAY

Eight days went by, eight days
Comforted by no nights, until finally:
"Would you behold yourself old, beloved?"
I was pierced, yet I consented gladly
For I knew it could not be otherwise.
And she—"Behold yourself old!
Sustained in strength, wielding might in gript surges!
Not bodying the sun in weak leaps
But holding way over rockish men
With fern free fingers on their little crags,
Their hollows, the new Atlas, to bear them
For pride and for mockery! Behold

Yourself old! winding with slow might—
A vine among oaks—to the thin tops:
Leaving the leafless leaved,
Bearing purple clusters! Behold
Yourself old! birds are behind you.
You are the wind coming that stills birds,
Shakes the leaves in booming polyphony—
Slow, winning high way amid the knocking
Of boughs, evenly crescendo,
The din and bellow of the male wind!
Leap then from forest into foam!
Lash about from low into high flames
Tipping sound, the female chorus—
Linking all lions, all twitterings
To make them nothing! Behold yourself old!"
As I made to answer she continued,
A little wistfully yet in a voice clear cut:
"Good is my overlip and evil
My underlip to you henceforth:
For I have taken your soul between my two hands
And this shall be as it is spoken."

ST. JAMES' GROVE

And so it came to that last day
When, she leading by the hand, we went out
Early in the morning, I heavy of heart
For I knew the novitiate was ended
The ecstasy was over, the life begun.

In my woolen shirt and the pale blue necktie
My grandmother gave me, there I went
With the old queen right past the houses

67

Of my friends down the hill to the river
As on any usual day, any errand.
Alone, walking under trees,
I went with her, she with me in her wild hair,
By Santiago Grove and presently
She bent forward and knelt by the river,
The Passaic, that filthy river.
And there dabbling her mad hands,
She called me close beside her.
Raising the water then in the cupped palm
She bathed our brows wailing and laughing:
"River, we are old, you and I,
We are old and by bad luck, beggars.
Lo, the filth in our hair, our bodies stink!
Old friend, here I have brought you
The young soul you long asked of me.
Stand forth, river, and give me
The old friend of my revels!
Give me the well-worn spirit,
For here I have made a room for it,
And I will return to you forthwith
The youth you have long asked of me:
Stand forth, river, and give me
The old friend of my revels!"

And the filthy Passaic consented!

Then she, leaping up with a fierce cry:
"Enter, youth, into this bulk!
Enter, river, into this young man!"
Then the river began to enter my heart,
Eddying back cool and limpid

Into the crystal beginning of its days.
But with the rebound it leaped forward:
Muddy, then black and shrunken
Till I felt the utter depth of its rottenness
The vile breadth of its degradation
And dropped down knowing this was me now.
But she lifted me and the water took a new tide
Again into the older experiences,
And so, backward and forward,
It tortured itself within me
Until time had been washed finally under,
And the river had found its level
And its last motion had ceased
And I knew all—it became me.
And I knew this for double certain
For there, whitely, I saw myself
Being borne off under the water!
I could have shouted out in my agony
At the sight of myself departing
Forever—but I bit back my despair
For she had averted her eyes
By which I knew well what she was thinking—
And so the last of me was taken.

Then she, "Be mostly silent!"
And turning to the river, spoke again:
"For him and for me, river, the wandering,
But by you I leave for happiness
Deep foliage, the thickest beeches—
Though elsewhere they are all dying—
Tallest oaks and yellow birches
That dip their leaves in you, mourning,

As now I dip my hair, immemorial
Of me, immemorial of him
Immemorial of these our promises!
Here shall be a bird's paradise,
They sing to you remembering my voice:
Here the most secluded spaces
For miles around, hallowed by a stench
To be our joint solitude and temple;
In memory of this clear marriage
And the child I have brought you in the late years.
Live, river, live in luxuriance
Remembering this our son,
In remembrance of me and my sorrow
And of the new wandering!"

I WANTED TO WRITE A POEM

AL QUE QUIERE!

This, the third book, also took $50 out of my pocket. Edmund R. Brown, publisher of the Four Seas Company in Boston, agreed to publish it. No, it was more than $50, but some of the money could be considered toward my fourth book, *Sour Grapes,* which the Four Seas Company also published with no further donation from me.

The figure on the cover was taken from a design on a pebble. To me the design looked like a dancer, and the effect of the dancer was very important—a natural, completely individual pattern. The artist made the outline around the design too geometrical; it should have been irregular, as the pebble was.

My translation of the phrase *Al Que Quiere!* is "To Him Who Wants It," and I have always associated it with a figure on a soccer field: to him who wants the ball to be passed to him. Moreover I associate it with a particular boy, older than myself, at school with me in 1898 at Château de Lançy near Geneva, Switzerland. He was a fine soccer player and he took me under his wing, got me on the varsity team. His name was Suares, a Spaniard, and as I was half-Spanish, there was a bond. He gave me his school cap when he left, a great honor. The phrase made me think of him, wanting the ball on the soccer field, and of

Excerpted from William Carlos Williams, *I Wanted to Write a Poem: The Autobiography of the Works of a Poet* (Beacon Press, 1958; New Directions, 1978), reported and edited by Edith Heal.

myself. I was convinced nobody in the world of poetry wanted me but I was there willing to pass the ball if anyone did want it.

Around 1914 I began to know other poets. The *Others* movement had started, originated by Walter Arensberg and Alfred Kreymborg. Alfred lived in Grantwood, New Jersey, all year round, in a shack never meant for winter. His wife Gertrude was very devoted and starry-eyed, married to a penniless poet but loving it. Believe me he made her work. I made weekly trips, winter and summer, to help read manuscripts, correct proofs. I finally edited one of the issues and probably paid for it. We published Maxwell Bodenheim. I liked him, felt he needed help; he stayed with Floss and me for awhile. Whenever I wrote at this time, the poems were written with *Others* in mind. I made no attempt to get publication anywhere else; the poems were definitely for *Others*. Except for the first published poems in the English magazine, *The Poetry Review*, some in another English magazine called *The Egoist*, and the few accepted by *Poetry*, *Others* got them all and, of course, we—myself and my friends—owned it, so you see I wasn't really cutting much of a figure as a poet.

I met Marianne Moore for the first time in the *Others* days. She had a head of the most glorious auburn hair and eyes—I don't even know to this day whether they were blue or green—but these features were about her only claim to physical beauty. We all loved and not a little feared her not only because of her keen wit but for her skill as a writer of poems. She had a unique style of her own; none of us wanted to copy it but we admired it. Her kindness to *Others* was not without barbs. Her loyalty to the group and to her mother was unflagging. It irritated us somewhat, the mother thing, but there was nothing to do about it.

Until my father's death, I turned to him with my literary

problems. We translated a short story from the Spanish to-
gether. It was by Rafael Arévalo Martínez, called "El hombre
que parecía un caballo." We had a great argument about the
English wording of the title. The literal translation appeared
to be "The Man Who Looked Like a Horse," but we weren't
satisfied. Finally it came to my father: "The Man Who Resem-
bled a Horse." It was a linguistic triumph which my father and
I shared.

I'd like to talk about some of the poems in *Al Que Quiere!*
Why did I use the Latin title *Sub Terra* for this poem? I was not
pretentious—yes, I guess I was. I thought I was contemptuous
of Latin but I suppose I wanted to appear as a Latin scholar
which I was not. The idea of the poem is this. I thought of
myself as being under the earth, buried in other words, but
as any plant is buried, retaining the power to come again. The
poem is Spring, the earth giving birth to a new crop of poets,
showing that I thought I would some day take my place among
them, telling them that I was coming pretty soon. See how ear-
nest and passionate about the idea I was? Look at the last line:
"nostrils lipping the wind!" Without knowing Greek I had read
translations of *The Odes of Theocritus* and felt myself very much
attracted by the pastoral mode. But my feeling for the country
was not as sophisticated as the pastorals with their picturesque
shepherdesses. I was always a country boy, felt myself a country
boy. To me the countryside was a real world but nonetheless a
poetic world. I have always had a feeling of identity with na-
ture, but not assertive; I have always believed in keeping myself
out of the picture. When I spoke of flowers, I *was* a flower, with
all the prerogatives of flowers, especially the right to come alive
in the Spring.

I was interested in the construction of an image before the
image was popular in poetry. The poem "Metric Figure" is an

example. I was influenced by my mother's still lifes. I was looking for a metric figure—a new measure. I couldn't find it and I couldn't wait for it. I was too impatient; I had to write.

"Woman Walking"—this is a poem about a poor person, the woman who brought us honey and eggs, a quite different figure from the lovely milkmaids of the pastorals, not at all the Marie Antoinette kind of thing.

"Gulls" is a study in sheer observation, a picture, a quiet poem, as most of the poems in *Al Que Quiere!* are. But it all presaged something. These gulls made a deep impression on me. *Paterson V* must be written, is being written, and the gulls appear at the beginning. Why must it be written? *Paterson IV* ends with the protagonist breaking through the bushes, identifying himself with the land, with America. He finally will die but it can't be categorically stated that death ends *anything*. When you're through with sex, with ambition, what can an old man create? Art, of course, a piece of art that will go beyond him into the lives of young people, the people who haven't had time to create. The old man meets the young people and lives on.

The poems are for the most part short, written in conversational language, as spoken, but rhythmical I think. The stanzas are short; I was searching for some formal arrangement of the lines, perhaps a stanzaic form. I have always had something to say and the sheer sense of what is spoken seemed to me all important, yet I knew the poem must have shape. From this time on you can see the struggle to get a form without deforming the language. In theme, the poems of *Al Que Quiere!* reflect things around me. I was finding out about life. Rather late, I imagine. This was a quiet period, a pre-sex period, although I was married. The "Love Song" addressed to my wife is cryptic, shy. I was trying to tell of the power of love, how it can uproot whole oaks.

"In Harbor," a short nature piece, was praised by Dorothy

Pound. She mentioned it in 1913. "M. B." is Maxwell Bodenheim, a theatrical figure to me. "Promenade" is about Billy, my son, when he was first born. I call him "sonny" in the poem.

"El Hombre"—"the man"—is only four short lines. Wallace Stevens wrote a letter praising it and used it as a first verse in one of his own poems. I was deeply touched.*

"Hero" is the military hero, not the romantic hero like Lord Byron. My hero has nothing to do with women in his heroic moments. He is facing danger, death. Female flesh is delicious but at this moment it doesn't concern him.

---

* The poem referred to is in *Harmonium,* by Wallace Stevens.

NUANCES OF A THEME BY WILLIAMS

It's a strange courage
you give me, ancient star:

Shine alone in the sunrise
toward which you lend no part!

I
Shine alone, shine nakedly, shine like bronze,
that reflects neither my face nor any inner part
of my being, shine like fire, that mirrors nothing.

II
Lend no part to any humanity that suffuses
you in its own light.
Be not chimera of morning,
Half-man, half-star.
Be not an intelligence,
Like a widow's bird
Or an old horse.

—From Wallace Stevens, *The Collected Poems*
of Wallace Stevens (Knopf, 1954).

"Canthara" is Spanish Fly and the legend about it. An old colored man, Mr. Marshall,* told me about it, how if you feed it to girls they go crazy and you'll get your desire, an insatiable woman. His description of them exposing all they had to the wind seemed to me an occasion for poetry, so I wrote the poem.

"Mujer"—our wonderful Mother Kitty. We had her twelve years, and when she was ready to die she just went quietly down in the cellar and lay on her side. She was beautiful. So beautiful we decided once to mate her with a thoroughbred. There was a $10 male and a $20 male. We thought we could afford the $10 male but they called us up and said that Mother Kitty would have nothing to do with him, tore him to pieces. She accepted the $20 male and proceeded to produce just one lone kitten. My, what spirit. The closing lines in the poem will tell you our constant Mother Kitty predicament: "and you return to us / in this condition."

"January Morning"—Marianne Moore liked it. "Tract" is the one people always ask me to read; I suppose because it has almost a narrative sequence. It's the one that begins: "I will teach you my townspeople / how to perform a funeral."

The titles of the poems tell you how I looked around me and saw something that suggested a poem: "Man with a Bad Heart," "Child," "The Old Men," "Dedication for a Plot of Ground."

"History" appears to be most impromptu but I worked a lot on it. It is perhaps the first example of a studied poem except for the very early poems which were studied in no uncertain terms when I was trying to imitate Keats. I was self-consciously talking about history and it showed.

---

* Thaddeus Marshall (1852–1930), owner of the red wheelbarrow that Williams made famous; see William Logan, "The Red Wheelbarrow," *Parnassus* 34.1/2 (2015): 204–231. —Ed.

The last long poem in *Al Que Quiere!*, "The Wanderer—a Rococo Study," was written before the other poems in the book [and first published in *The Egoist* in 1914]. Why *Rococo* I don't know except it was one of my mother's favorite words. It is actually a reconstruction from memory of my early Keatsian *Endymion* imitation that I destroyed, burned in a furnace! It is the story of growing up. The old woman in it is my grandmother, raised to heroic proportions. I endowed her with magic qualities. She had seized me from my mother as her special possession, adopted me, and her purpose in life was to make me her own. But my mother ended all that with a terrific slap in the puss.

In *The Complete Collected Poems of William Carlos Williams, 1906–1938* (New Directions, 1938), Williams presented another version of *Al Que Quiere!* He rearranged the sequence of the poems dramatically, in addition to omitting eight poems ("Woman Walking"; "Appeal"; "Foreign"; "History"; "Portrait of a Young Man with a Bad Heart"; "Invitation"; "Divertimiento"; "The Wanderer") and including four other poems written during 1915 and 1916 ("Spring Song"; "The Shadow"; "The Young Housewife"; "Drink"), all four of which can be found in *The Collected Poems of William Carlos Williams, 1909–1939* (New Directions, 1986). —Ed.

THE MAN WHO RESEMBLED A HORSE

by Rafael Arévalo Martínez

translated from the Spanish by William Carlos Williams

At the time we were presented he was at one end of the apartment, his head on one side, as horses are accustomed to stand, with an air as if unconscious of all going on around him. He had long, stiff, and dried-out limbs, strangely put together, like those of one of the characters in an English illustration of *Gulliver's Travels*. But my impression that the man in some mysterious way resembled a horse was not obtained then, except in a subconscious manner, which might never have risen to the full life of consciousness had not my abnormal contact with the hero of this story been prolonged.

In this very first scene of our introduction Señor de Aretal began by way of welcome to exhibit the translucent strings of opals, amethysts, emeralds, and carbuncles which constituted his intimate treasure. In a first moment of dazzlement I spread myself out; I opened myself completely like a great white sheet, in order to make greater my surface of contact with the generous giver. The antennae of my soul went out, felt him and returned, tremulous, moved, delighted to give me the good news: "This is the man you awaited; this is the man in search of whom you peered into all unknown souls, for your intuition had affirmed to you long since that some day you would be enriched

Originally published in *The Little Review* 5.8 (Dec. 1918): 42–53; and subsequently, revised and with note on the translation by Williams, in *New Directions in Prose and Poetry* 8 (1944): 309–319. —Ed.

by the advent of a unique being. The avidity with which you have seized, stared into, and cast aside so many souls which made themselves desired and deceived your hope shall today be amply satisfied: Stoop and drink of this water."

And when he arose to go, I followed him, tied and a captive, like the lamb which the shepherdess bound with garlands of roses. Once in the living room of my new friend, having no more than crossed the threshold which gave him passage to a propitious and habitual environment, his entire person burst into flame. He became dazzling, picturesque as the horse of an emperor in a military parade. The skirts of his coat had a vague resemblance to the inner tunic of a steed of the Middle Ages harnessed for a tournament. They fell below his meager buttocks, caressing his fine and distinguished thighs. And his theatrical performance began.

After a ritual of preparation carefully observed—knight initiate of a most ancient cult—and when our souls had already become concave, he brought forth his folio of verses with the unctuous deportment of a priest who draws near the altar. He was so grave that he imposed respect. A laugh would have been put to the knife in the instant of its birth.

He drew forth his first string of topazes, or, better said, his first series of strings of topazes, translucent and brilliant. His hands were raised with such cadence that the rhythm extended three worlds removed. By the power of the rhythm our room was moved entire to the second floor, like a captive balloon, until it broke free from its earthly ties and carried us on a silent aerial journey. But I was not won by his verses for they were inorganic. They were the translucid and radiant soul of minerals; they were the symmetrical and flinty soul of minerals.

And then the officiant of mineral things brought forth his second necklace. Oh emeralds, divine emeralds! And he showed the third. Oh diamonds, clear diamonds! And he brought the fourth and the fifth, which were again topazes like drops of light, with accumulations from the sun, with parts opaquely radiant. And then the seventh: his carbuncles! His carbuncles were—almost warm; they nearly moved me as might pomegranate seeds or the blood of heroes; but I touched them and I felt them hard. By every means the soul of mineral things invaded me; that inorganic aristocracy seduced me strangely, without my fully comprehending. So much was this true that I could not translate the words of my inner master who was confused and made a vain effort to become hard and symmetrical and limited and brilliant; I remained dumb. And then, in an unforeseen explosion of offended dignity, believing himself deceived, the officiant took from me his necklace of carbuncles with a movement so full of violence but so just that it left me more perplexed than hurt. If it had been he of the roses he would not have acted in this way.

And then, as upon the breaking of a charm by that act of violence, the enchantment of the rhythm was shattered; and the little white boat in which we had been flying through the blue of the sky found itself solidly planted on the first floor of the house.

Later, our mutual friend, Señor de Aretal and I lunched together on the lower floor of the hotel.

In these moments I looked into the well of the soul of the master of the topazes. I saw many things reflected. As I looked in I had instinctively spread my peacock's tail; but I had spread it without an inner sense of the thing; simply urged by so much beauty perceived and desiring to show my best aspect in order to place myself in tone with it.

Oh, the things I saw in that well! The well was for me the very well of mystery itself. To look into a human soul, wide

81

open as a well, which is an eye of the earth, is the same thing as to get a glimpse of God. We never can see the bottom. But we saturate ourselves in the moisture of the water, the great vehicle of love; and we are bedazzled with reflected light.

This well reflected the multiple external aspect of things in the very manner of Señor de Aretal. Certain figures showed more clearly than others on the surface of the water: there were reflected the classics—that treasure of tenderness and wisdom, the classics; but above all there was reflected the image of an absent friend with such purity of line and such exact coloring that the fact that this parallel should give me knowledge of the soul of *el Señor de la Rosa*, the absent friend so admired and so loved, was not one of the least interesting attractions which the soul of Señor de Aretal possessed for me. Above all else there was reflected God. God, from whom I was never less distant. The great soul which for a time is brought into focus. I understood as I looked into the well of Señor de Aretal that he was a divine messenger. He brought a message to humanity—the human message, which has the greatest value of all. But he was an unconscious messenger. He lavished good, but he had it not in his possession.

Soon I interested my noble host to an unusual degree. I leant over the clear water of his spirit with such avidity that he was enabled to get a clear likeness of me. I had drawn sufficiently near and besides I was in addition a clear thing which did not intercept the light. Possibly I obscured him as much as he did me. It is a quality of things brought under hallucination to be in their turn hallucinators. This mutual attraction drew us together and brought us into intimate relationship. I frequented the divine temple of that beautiful soul. At its contact I began to take fire. Señor de Aretal was a lighted lamp and I was stuff ready to burn. Our souls communicated with each other. I held my hands extended and the soul of each one of my ten fingers was an antenna through which I received the knowledge of the soul of Señor de Aretal. Thus I became aware of many things unknown before. Through aerial routes—what else are the fingers, or velvety leaves, for what else but aerial routes are the leaves—I received something from that man which had been lacking me till that time. *I had been an adventurous shrub which prolongs its filaments until it finds the necessary humus in new earth. And how I fed! I fed with the joy of tremulous leaves of chlorophyll that spread themselves to the sun; with the joy with which a root encounters a decomposing corpse; with the joy with which convalescents take their vacillating steps in the light-flooded mornings of spring;* with the joy with which a child clings to the nutritious breast and afterward, being full, smiles in his dreams at the vision of a snowy udder. Bah! All things which complete themselves have had that joy. God, some day, will be nothing more than a food for us: something needed for our life. Thus smile children and the young when they feel themselves gratified by nutrition.

Beyond that I took fire. Nutrition is combustion. Who knows what divine child shook over my spirit a sprinkling of gunpowder, of naphtha, of something easily inflammable; and Señor de Aretal, who had known how to draw near me, had set fire to it. I had the pleasure of burning, that is to say, of fulfilling my destiny. I understood that I was a thing easily inflammable. Oh, father fire, blessed be thou! My destiny is to burn. Fire is also a message. What other souls will take fire from me? To whom would I communicate my flame? Bah! Who can foretell the future of a spark?

I burnt and Señor de Aretal saw me burn. In marvelous harmony our two atoms of hydrogen and oxygen had approached so closely that, stretching themselves, throwing out particles,

---

*   Epigraph of *Al Que Quiere!* —Ed.

they almost succeeded in uniting into a living thing. At times they fluttered about like two butterflies which seek each other and make marvelous loops over the river and in the air. At other times they rose by virtue of their own rhythm and harmonious consonance, as rise the two wings of a distich. One was impregnating the other. Until …

Have you heard of those icebergs which, drawn into warm waters by a submarine current, disintegrate at their base until, the marvelous equilibrium being lost, they revolve upon themselves in an apocalyptic turning, rapid, unforeseen, presenting to the face of the sun what had before been hidden beneath the sea? Inverted they appear unconscious of the ships which, when their upper part went under, they caused to sink into the abyss. Unconscious of the loss of nests which had been built in their parts heretofore turned to the light, in the relative stability of those two fragile things: eggs and ice.

Thus, suddenly, there began to take shape in the transparent angel of Señor de Aretal a dark, little, almost insubstantial cloud. It was the projected shadow of the horse that was drawing near.

Who could express my grief when there appeared in the angel of Señor de Aretal that thing—obscure, vague, and formless. My noble friend had gone down to the bar of the hotel in which he lived. Who was passing? Bah! A dark thing possessed of a horrible flattened nose and thin lips. Do you understand? If the line of the nose had been straight then also something would have been straightened in his soul. If his lips had been full, his sincerity would have been increased also. But no. Señor de Aretal had called him. There he was … And my soul which at that instant had power to discern clearly understood that that dwarf whom I had until then thought to be a man, since I one day saw his cheeks color with shame, was no more than a pygmy. With such nostrils one could not be sincere.

Invited by the master of the topazes we seated ourselves at a table. They served us cognac and refreshments to take or leave. Here the harmony was broken. The alcohol broke it. I did not take any. He drank. But the alcohol was near me on the white marble table. It came between us and intercepted our souls. Furthermore, the soul of Señor de Aretal was no longer blue like mine. It was red and flat like that of the companion who separated us. Then I understood that what I had most loved in Señor de Aretal was my own blue.

Soon the flattened soul of Señor de Aretal began to speak of low things. All his thoughts had the crooked nose. All his thoughts drank alcohol and materialized grossly. He told us of a legion of Jamaican negresses, lewd and semi-naked, pursuing him with the offer of their odious merchandise for a nickel. His speech pained me, and soon his will pained me. He asked me insistently to drink alcohol. I yielded. But hardly had my sacrifice been consummated then I felt clearly that something was breaking between us—that our inner masters were withdrawing and that a divine equilibrium of crystals was tumbling down in silence. I told him so: "Señor de Aretal, you have broken our divine relationship in this very instant. Tomorrow you will see me arrive at your apartment, a man only, and I will meet only a man in you. In this very instant you have dyed me in red."

The following day in effect, I do not know what we did, Señor de Aretal and I. I believe we were walking along the street bent upon some sort of business. He was again ablaze. I was walking at his side extinguished and far removed. As I walked I was thinking to myself that mystery had never opened so wide a slit for me to look through as in my relations with my strange fellow voyager. I had never felt so thoroughly the possibilities of man; I had never so well understood the intimate God as in my relations with Señor de Aretal.

We arrived at his room. His forms of thought were awaiting us. And all the while I felt myself far from Señor de Aretal. I felt far for many days, on many successive visits. I went to him, obeying inexorable laws. Because precisely that contact was required to consume a part in me, so dry until then, as if prepared the better to burn. All my pain of dryness hitherto now rejoiced in burning; all the pain of my emptiness hitherto now rejoiced in fullness. I sallied out of the night of my soul into a blazing dawn. It is well. Let us be brave. The dryer we are the better we shall burn. And so I went to that man and our inner masters rejoiced. Ah! but the enchantment of the first days. Now where?

When I had become resigned to find a man in Señor de Aretal, there returned anew the enchantment of his marvelous presence. I loved my friend. But it was impossible for me to throw aside the melancholy of the departed god. Translucid, diamantine lost wings! How might I recover them and return where we were?

One day Señor de Aretal found the medium propitious. We his hearers were several; verses were being recited in the room enchanted by his habitual creations. Suddenly, in the presence of some more beautiful than the rest, as upon a horn blast, our noble host arose pawing and prancing. And then and there I had my first vision: *Señor de Aretal stretched his neck like a horse.*

I attracted his attention: "Worthy host, I beg you to take this and this attitude." Yes; it was true: *he stretched his neck like a horse.*

Later; the second vision; the same day. We went out to walk. Of a sudden I perceived, I perceived it: *Señor de Aretal fell like a horse.* Suddenly his left foot gave way, then his haunches nearly touched the ground, like a horse that stumbles. He recovered himself quickly; but he had already given me the impression. Have you seen a horse fall?

Then the third vision, a few days later. Señor de Aretal was performing, seated before his money in gold; suddenly I saw him move his arms as horses of pure blood move their forefeet, thrusting the extremities of their legs forward, to either side, in that beautiful series of movements which you doubtless have many times observed when an able rider in a crowded thoroughfare curbs the pace of his curvetting and splendid mount.

Afterward another vision: Señor de Aretal looked at things like a horse. When he was drunk with his own words, as his own generous blood makes a high-bred steed drunk, tremulous as a leaf—trembling like a steed mounted and curbed, trembling like all living forms of nervous and fine fiber—he would bend down his head, he would turn his head sidewise, and thus he looked about, while his arms knitted something in the air, like the forepaws of a horse. What a magnificent thing a horse is! He almost stands upon two feet! And then I felt that the spirit was riding him.

And later a hundred visions more. Señor de Aretal approached women like a horse. In sumptuous parlors he could not remain quiet. He would draw alongside some lovely woman, newly introduced, with elastic and easy movements, bow his head and hold it on the side; he would take a turn around her and take a turn around the room.

Thus he looked sidelong. I was able to observe that his eyes were bloodshot. One day he broke one of the small vessels which color them with a delicate network: the little vessel broke and a tiny red stain colored his sclera. I called it to his attention.

"Bah," said he to me, "that is an old matter. I have suffered with it for three days. But have no time to see a doctor."

He walked to a glass and looked into it fixedly. When I returned on the following day, I found that one more virtue ennobled him. I asked him: "What beautifies you in this hour?"

And he replied: "A hue." And he told me that he had put on a red necktie that it might harmonize with his red eye. Then I understood that there was in his spirit a third red and that these three reds together were what had attracted my attention when saluting him. For the crystal spirit of Señor de Aretal was wont to take on the hue of surrounding things. And this is what his verses were: a marvelous collection of crystals tinged by the things about them: emeralds, rubies, opals ...

But this was at times sad because at times surrounding things were dark or discolored: the greens of the manure pile, the pale greens of sickly plants. I came to deplore finding him with others and when this happened I would leave Señor de Aretal under any pretext if his companion were not a person of clear colors.

For unfailingly Señor de Aretal reflected the spirit of his companion. One day I found him, he the noble steed! dwarfed and honeyed. And as in a mirror, I saw in the room a person dwarfed and honeyed. Sure enough, there she was: he presented her. A woman flattened, fat and low. Her spirit likewise was a low thing. Something trailing and humble; but inoffensive and desirous of pleasing. That person was the spirit of flattery. And Señor de Aretal also at that moment possessed a small soul, servile and obsequious. What convex mirror has brought about this horrible transformation? I asked myself, terrified. And at once all the air of the room appeared to me as a transparent convex glass which distorted the objects. How flattened the chairs were...! Everything offered itself to be sat upon. Aretal was one hack horse the more.

On another occasion, at the table of a noisy group which laughed and drank, Aretal was one human the more, one more of the heap. I drew alongside him and saw him listed and the price fixed. He cracked jokes and brandished them like weapons of defense. He was a circus horse. All in that group were on exhibition. Another time he was a *jayán*.* He entangled himself in abusive words with a brute of a man. He was like a market woman. He would have disgusted me; but I loved him so much that it made me sad. He was a kicking horse.

Finally there appeared on the physical plane a question which I had long been shaping: which is the true spirit of Señor de Aretal? And I answered it quickly. Señor de Aretal with his fine mentality had no soul: he was amoral. He was amoral as a horse and allowed himself to be mounted by any spirit whatever. At times his riders were fearful or miserly and then Señor de Aretal would fling them from him with a proud buck. That moral vacuum of his being would fill, as do all vacuums, with ease. It tended to fill itself.

I proposed the question to the very exalted mind of my friend and he took it up at once. He made me a confession: "Yes: it is true. I show you who love me the better part of me. I show you my inner god. But, it is painful to say it, between two human beings around me I tend to take on the color of the lower. Flee from me when I am in bad company."

Upon the base of this discovery I entered still more deeply into his spirit. He confessed to me one day, in grief, that no woman had ever loved him. All his being bled as he said this. I explained to him that no woman could love him, because he was not a man; the union would have been monstrous. Señor de Aretal did not know modesty and was indelicate in his relations with ladies, like an animal. And he:

—But I heap them with money.

—That also would be given them by a valuable property rented.

And he:

—But I caress them with passion.

---

* Foul-mouthed cuss. —Ed.

—Their little wooly dogs also lick their hands.

And he:

—But I am faithful and generous to them; I am humble to them; I am self-denying to them.

—Well; man is more than that. But, do you love them?

—Yes, I love them.

—But do you love them as a man? No, friend, no. You break in those delicate and divine beings a thousand slender cords which constitute a life entire. That last prostitute, who denied you her love and has disdained your money, defended her one inviolate part: her inner master; that which is not sold. You have no shame. Now listen to my prophecy: a woman will redeem you. You, obsequious and humble to lowliness with the ladies; you proud to carry a lovely woman, on your back, with the pride of the favorite nag which delights in its burden—when this beautiful woman shall love you, you will be redeemed; you will acquire chastity by conquest.

And at another time propitious for confidences.

—I have never had a friend. And his entire being bled as he said this. I explained to him that no man could give him his friendship because he was not a man, and the friendship would have been monstrous. Señor de Aretal did not comprehend friendship and was indelicate in his relations with men, like an animal. He knew only comradeship. He galloped joyful and openhearted upon the plain with his companions; he liked to go in droves with them; primitive and primordial he galloped, feeling the burning of his generous blood which incited him to action—becoming drunk with the air, the verdure and the sun; but later he would withdraw with indifference from his companion of a year. The horse, his brother dead beside him, sees him rot beneath the dome of the heavens without a tear rising to his eyes ... And Señor de Aretal, when I had finished expressing my last concept, radiant:

—This is the glory of nature. Matter, immortal, does not die. Why weep for a horse when a rose remains? Why weep for a rose when a bird is there? Why lament for a friend when a meadow remains? I feel the radiant light of the sun which possesses us all, which redeems us all. To weep is to sin against the sun. Men, cowards, miserable and low, sin against nature, which is God.

And I, reverent, on my knees before that beautiful animal soul which filled me with the unction of God:

—Yes, it is true; but man is a part of nature; he is nature evolved. I respect evolution! There is force and there is matter; I respect them both! They are all one.

—I am beyond the moral.

—You are on this side of morality; you are below the moral. But the horse and the angel touch one another, and for this reason you at times appear to me as divine. St. Francis d'Assisi, like you, loved all beings and all things; but that being true, he loved them in another manner; he loved them beyond the circle, not this side of it as you do.

And then he:

—I am generous with my friends: I shower them with gold.

—It would also be given them by a valuable property leased, or by an oil well, or a working mine.

And he:

—But I pay them a thousand little attentions. I have been nurse to the sick friend and a boon companion in an orgy to the hale friend.

And I:

—Man is more than that; man is solidarity. You love your friends but do you love them with human love? No; you offended in us a thousand intangible things. I, who am the first man who has loved you, have sown the germ of your redemption. That egoistic friend who separated himself, in leaving you, from a benefactor, did not feel himself united to you by any human bond. You have no solidarity with men.

—......

—You have not modesty with women nor solidarity with men nor respect for the law. You lie, and find in your exalted mentality an excuse for your lie, although you are by nature truthful, like a horse. You flatter and deceive and find in your exalted mentality an excuse for your flattery and your deceit, although you are by nature noble, like a horse. I have never so loved horses as I love them in you. I understand the nobility of the horse: it is nearly human. You have always borne a human load upon your back: a woman, a friend ... What would become of that woman and that friend in the difficult passes without you, the noble, the strong, who bore them upon himself with a generosity which will be your redemption! He who bears a burden covers the road most swiftly. But you have borne them like a horse. Faithful to your nature, begin to bear them like a man.

I took leave of the master of the topazes and a few days later there occurred the last act of our relationship. Of a sudden Señor de Aretal sensed that my hand was unsteady, that it was held out to him in a cowardly and ungenerous manner and his nobility of the brute revolted. With a swift kick he threw me far from him. I felt his hoofs on my forehead. Then a rapid gallop, rhythmic and martial, scattering to the winds the sands of the desert. I turned my eyes toward the place where the sphinx had stood in her eternal repose of mystery and I no longer saw her. The sphinx was Señor de Aretal who had revealed to me his secret which was the same as that of the centaur!

It was Señor de Aretal, drawing away at a rapid gallop, with a human face and the body of a beast.

GUATEMALA, OCTOBER 1914

*BILINGUAL EDITION

For a complete listing, request a free catalog from New Directions, 80 8th Avenue, New York, NY 10011 or visit us online at **ndbooks.com**